BOOT CUFFS &
EAR WARMERS

Five sets offer a variety of stylish looks!

LEISURE ARTS, INC. • Little Rock, Arkansas

CROSS STITCH SET

 **EASY**

SHOPPING LIST

Yarn (Medium Weight)
[6 ounces, 315 yards
(170 grams, 288 meters) per skein]:
☐   2 skeins

Crochet Hook
☐   Size H (5 mm) **or** size needed for gauge

SIZE INFORMATION

Cuff - 5½" high x 13" circumference (14 cm x 33 cm)
Ear Warmer - 3½" wide x 18¼" circumference (9 cm x 46 cm)

GAUGE INFORMATION

In pattern, 6 Cross Sts = 4" (10 cm);
Rnds 1-7 = 2¾" (7 cm)

Gauge Swatch: 3" (7.5 cm) square
Ch 14.

Row 1: Hdc in third ch from hook
and in each ch across **(2 skipped
chs count as first hdc)**: 13 hdc.

Rows 2-9: Ch 2 **(counts as first
hdc)**, turn; (work FPhdc around
next st, work BPhdc around next
st) across.

Finish off.

─── STITCH GUIDE ───

TREBLE CROCHET
(abbreviated tr)

YO twice, insert hook in st
indicated, YO and pull up a loop
(4 loops on hook), (YO and draw
through 2 loops on hook) 3 times.

FRONT POST HALF DOUBLE
CROCHET *(abbreviated FPhdc)*

YO, insert hook from **front** to **back**
around post of st indicated *(Fig. 3,
page 45)*, YO and pull up a loop,
YO and draw through all 3 loops
on hook.

BACK POST HALF DOUBLE
CROCHET *(abbreviated BPhdc)*

YO, insert hook from **back** to **front**
around post of st indicated *(Fig. 3,
page 45)*, YO and pull up a loop,
YO and draw through all 3 loops
on hook.

CROSS ST (uses next 3 sts)

Skip next 2 sts, tr in next st, ch 1,
working **around** tr just made, tr in
first skipped st.

INSTRUCTIONS
Cuff (Make 2)

Beginning at bottom edge, ch 58; being careful **not** to twist ch, join with slip st to form a ring.

Rnd 1 (Right side)**:** Ch 2 (**counts as first hdc, now and throughout**), hdc in next ch and in each ch around; join with slip st to first hdc: 58 hdc.

Rnd 2: Ch 2, work FPhdc around next hdc, ★ work BPdc around next hdc, work FPhdc around next hdc; repeat from ★ around; join with slip st to first hdc.

Rnd 3: Ch 2, work FPhdc around next FPhdc, ★ work BPhdc around next BPhdc, work FPhdc around next FPhdc; repeat from ★ around; join with slip st to first hdc.

Rnd 4: Ch 2, work Cross Sts around; join with slip st to first hdc: 19 Cross Sts and one hdc.

Rnd 5: Ch 1, sc in same st as joining and in each st and each ch-1 sp around; join with slip st to first sc: 58 sc.

Rnds 6-9: Repeat Rnds 4 and 5 twice: 58 sc.

Rnd 10: Ch 2, hdc in next sc and in each sc around; join with slip st to first hdc.

Rnd 11: Ch 2, work FPhdc around next hdc, ★ work BPdc around next hdc, work FPhdc around next hdc; repeat from ★ around; join with slip st to first hdc.

Rnds 12-15: Repeat Rnd 3, 4 times.

Finish off.

Ear Warmer

Ch 82; being careful **not** to twist ch, join with slip st to form a ring.

Rnd 1 (Right side)**:** Ch 2 **(counts as first hdc, now and throughout)**, hdc in next ch and in each ch around; join with slip st to first hdc: 82 hdc.

Rnd 2: Ch 2, work FPhdc around next hdc, ★ work BPdc around next hdc, work FPhdc around next hdc; repeat from ★ around; join with slip st to first hdc.

Rnd 3: Ch 2, work FPhdc around next FPhdc, ★ work BPhdc around next BPhdc, work FPhdc around next FPhdc; repeat from ★ around; join with slip st to first hdc.

Rnd 4: Ch 2, work Cross Sts around; join with slip st to first hdc: 27 Cross Sts and one hdc.

Rnd 5: Ch 1, sc in same st as joining and in each st and each ch-1 sp around; join with slip st to first sc: 82 sc.

Rnds 6 and 7: Repeat Rnds 4 and 5: 82 sc.

Rnd 8: Ch 2, hdc in next sc and in each sc around; join with slip st to first hdc.

Rnds 9 and 10: Repeat Rnds 2 and 3.

Finish off.

IRISH SEA SET

□■■□□□ **EASY +**

SHOPPING LIST

Yarn (Medium Weight)

[7 ounces, 364 yards

(198 grams, 333 meters) per skein]:

☐ 1 skein

Crochet Hook

☐ Size H (5 mm) **or** size needed for gauge

SIZE INFORMATION

Cuffs - 5½" high x 13" circumference (14 cm x 33 cm)

Ear Warmer - 3" wide x 18½" circumference (7.5 cm x 47 cm)

GAUGE INFORMATION

In pattern, 13 sts and 9 rows/rnds = 3" (7.5 cm)

Gauge Swatch: 3" (7.5 cm) square

Ch 14.

Row 1: Hdc in third ch from hook and in each ch across (**2 skipped chs count as first hdc**): 13 hdc.

Rows 2-9: Ch 2 (**counts as first hdc**), turn; (work FPhdc around next st, work BPhdc around next st) across.

Finish off.

STITCH GUIDE

FRONT POST HALF DOUBLE CROCHET *(abbreviated FPhdc)*

YO, insert hook from **front** to **back** around post of st indicated *(Fig. 3, page 45)*, YO and pull up a loop, YO and draw through all 3 loops on hook.

BACK POST HALF DOUBLE CROCHET *(abbreviated BPhdc)*

YO, insert hook from **back** to **front** around post of st indicated *(Fig. 3, page 45)*, YO and pull up a loop (3 loops on hook), YO and draw through all 3 loops on hook.

FRONT POST DOUBLE CROCHET *(abbreviated FPdc)*

YO, insert hook from **front** to **back** around post of st indicated *(Fig. 3, page 45)*, YO and pull up a loop (3 loops on hook), (YO and draw through 2 loops on hook) twice.

BACK POST DOUBLE CROCHET *(abbreviated BPdc)*

YO, insert hook from **back** to **front** around post of st indicated *(Fig. 3, page 45)*, YO and pull up a loop, (YO and draw through 2 loops on hook) twice.

SHELL (uses one st or sp)

(2 Dc, ch 1, 2 dc) in st or sp indicated.

INSTRUCTIONS
Cuff (Make 2)

Beginning at bottom edge, ch 56; being careful **not** to twist ch, join with slip st to form a ring.

Rnd 1 (Right side)**:** Ch 2 **(counts as first hdc, now and throughout)**, hdc in next ch and in each ch around; join with slip st to first hdc: 56 hdc.

Rnds 2-5: Ch 2, work FPhdc around next st, ★ work BPhdc around next st, work FPhdc around next st; repeat from ★ around; join with slip st to first hdc.

Rnd 6: Ch 3 **(counts as first dc, now and throughout)**, dc in next 2 sts, skip next 2 sts, work Shell in next st, skip next 2 sts, ★ dc in next 3 sts, skip next 2 sts, work Shell in next st, skip next 2 sts; repeat from ★ around; join with slip st to first dc.

Rnds 7-12: Ch 3, work FPdc around each of next 2 sts, work Shell in next ch-1 sp, skip next 2 sts, ★ work FPdc around each of next 3 sts, work Shell in next ch-1 sp, skip next 2 sts; repeat from ★ around; join with slip st to first dc.

Rnd 13: Ch 2, hdc in next FPdc and in each st and each ch-1 sp around; join with slip st to first hdc: 56 hdc.

Rnds 14-16: Ch 2, work FPhdc around next st, ★ work BPhdc around next st, work FPhdc around next st; repeat from ★ around; join with slip st to first hdc.

Finish off.

Ear Warmer

Ch 80; being careful **not** to twist ch, join with slip st to form a ring.

Rnd 1 (Right side)**:** Ch 2 **(counts as first hdc, now and throughout)**, hdc in next ch and in each ch around; join with slip st to first hdc: 80 hdc.

Rnd 2: Ch 2, work FPhdc around next hdc, ★ work BPhdc around next hdc, work FPhdc around next hdc; repeat from ★ around; join with slip st to first hdc.

Rnd 3: Ch 2, work FPhdc around next FPhdc, ★ work BPhdc around next BPhdc, work FPhdc around next FPhdc; repeat from ★ around; join with slip st to first hdc.

Rnd 4: Ch 3 **(counts as first dc, now and throughout)**, dc in next 2 sts, skip next 2 sts, work Shell in next st, skip next 2 sts, ★ dc in next 3 sts, skip next 2 sts, work Shell in next st, skip next 2 sts; repeat from ★ around; join with slip st to first dc.

Rnd 5: Ch 3, work FPdc around each of next 2 dc, work Shell in next ch-1 sp, skip next 2 dc, ★ work FPdc around each of next 3 dc, work Shell in next ch-1 sp, skip next 2 dc; repeat from ★ around; join with slip st to first dc.

Rnd 6: Ch 3, work FPdc around each of next 2 FPdc, work Shell in next ch-1 sp, ★ work FPdc around each of next 3 FPdc, work Shell in next ch-1 sp; repeat from ★ around; join with slip st to first dc.

Rnd 7: Ch 2, hdc in next FPdc and in each st and each ch-1 sp around; join with slip st to first hdc: 80 hdc.

Rnds 8 and 9: Repeat Rnds 2 and 3.

Finish off.

RIBBED SET

 **EASY**

SHOPPING LIST

Yarn (Medium Weight)

[7 ounces, 364 yards
(198 grams, 333 meters) per skein]:

☐ 1 skein

Crochet Hook

☐ Size H (5 mm) **or** size needed for gauge

SIZE INFORMATION

Cuff - 5½" high x 13" circumference (14 cm x 33 cm)
Ear Warmer - 3½" wide x 19" circumference (9 cm x 48.5 cm)

GAUGE INFORMATION

In pattern, 13 sts = 3" (7.5 cm);
    11 rows/rnds = 3½" (9 cm)
Gauge Swatch: 3" x 3½"
    (7.5 cm x 9 cm)
Ch 14.

Row 1: Hdc in third ch from hook and in each ch across **(2 skipped chs count as first hdc)**: 13 hdc.

Rows 2-11: Ch 2 **(counts as first hdc)**, turn; ★ work FPhdc around next st, work BPhdc around next st; repeat from ★ across.
Finish off.

—— STITCH GUIDE ——

FRONT POST HALF DOUBLE CROCHET *(abbreviated FPhdc)*
YO, insert hook from **front** to **back** around post of st indicated *(Fig. 3, page 45)*, YO and pull up a loop, YO and draw through all 3 loops on hook.

BACK POST HALF DOUBLE CROCHET *(abbreviated BPhdc)*
YO, insert hook from **back** to **front** around post of st indicated *(Fig. 3, page 45)*, YO and pull up a loop, YO and draw through all 3 loops on hook.

INSTRUCTIONS
Cuff (Make 2)

Beginning at bottom edge, ch 56; being careful **not** to twist ch, join with slip st to form a ring.

Rnd 1 (Right side)**:** Ch 2 (**counts as first hdc, now and throughout**), hdc in next ch and in each ch around; join with slip st to first hdc: 56 hdc.

Rnd 2: Ch 2, work FPhdc around next hdc, ★ work BPhdc around next hdc, work FPhdc around next hdc; repeat from ★ around; join with slip st to first hdc.

Rnds 3-20: Ch 2, work FPhdc around next FPhdc, ★ work BPhdc around next BPhdc, work FPhdc around next FPhdc; repeat from ★ around; join with slip st to first hdc.

Finish off.

Ear Warmer

Ch 82; being careful **not** to twist ch, join with slip st to form a ring.

Rnd 1 (Right side)**:** Ch 2 (**counts as first hdc, now and throughout**), hdc in next ch and in each ch around; join with slip st to first hdc: 82 hdc.

Rnd 2: Ch 2, work FPhdc around next hdc, ★ work BPhdc around next hdc, work FPhdc around next hdc; repeat from ★ around; join with slip st to first hdc.

Rnds 3-11: Ch 2, work FPhdc around next FPhdc, ★ work BPdc around next BPhdc, work FPhdc around next FPhdc; repeat from ★ around; join with slip st to first hdc.

Finish off.

RUFFLED SET

 **EASY**

SIZE INFORMATION

Cuffs - 5" high x 12½" circumference (12.5 cm x 32 cm)

Ear Warmer - 3¾" wide x 19" circumference (9.5 cm x 48.5 cm)

GAUGE INFORMATION

In pattern, 11 sts = 3" (7.5 cm); 9 rows/rnds = 3¾" (9.5 cm)

Gauge Swatch: 3" x 3¾" (7.5 cm x 9 cm)

Ch 12.

Row 1: Hdc in third ch from hook and in each ch across

(2 skipped chs count as first hdc): 11 hdc.

Rows 2-9: Ch 2 **(counts as first hdc)**, turn; ★ work FPhdc around next st, work BPhdc around next st; repeat from ★ across.

Finish off.

─── STITCH GUIDE ───

FRONT POST HALF DOUBLE CROCHET *(abbreviated FPhdc)*

YO, insert hook from **front** to **back** around post of st indicated *(Fig. 3, page 45)*, YO and pull up a loop, YO and draw through all 3 loops on hook.

BACK POST HALF DOUBLE CROCHET *(abbreviated BPhdc)*

YO, insert hook from **back** to **front** around post of st indicated *(Fig. 3, page 45)*, YO and pull up a loop, YO and draw through all 3 loops on hook.

2-DC CLUSTER (uses one st or sp)

★ YO, insert hook in st or sp indicated, YO and pull up a loop, YO and draw through 2 loops on hook; repeat from ★ once **more**, YO and draw through all 3 loops on hook.

ENDING 2-DC CLUSTER (uses one st)

YO, insert hook in same st as first hdc, YO and pull up a loop, YO and draw through 2 loops on hook (2 loops on hook), insert hook in first hdc, YO and pull up a loop, YO and draw through all 3 loops on hook.

INSTRUCTIONS
Cuff (Make 2)

Beginning at bottom edge, ch 46; being careful **not** to twist ch, join with slip st to form a ring.

Rnd 1 (Right side)**:** Ch 2 **(counts as first hdc, now and throughout)**, hdc in next ch and in each ch around; join with slip st to first hdc: 46 hdc.

Rnd 2: Ch 2, work FPhdc around next hdc, ★ work BPhdc around next hdc, work FPhdc around next hdc; repeat from ★ around; join with slip st to first hdc.

Rnd 3: Ch 2, work FPhdc around next FPhdc, ★ work BPhdc around next BPhdc, work FPhdc around next FPhdc; repeat from ★ around; join with slip st to first hdc.

Rnd 4: Ch 3 **(counts as first hdc plus ch 1, now and throughout)**, skip next FPhdc, ★ work 2-dc Cluster in next BPhdc, ch 1, skip next FPhdc; repeat from ★ around, work ending 2-dc Cluster: 23 Clusters and 23 ch-1 sps.

Rnds 5-9: Ch 3, (work 2-dc Cluster in next ch-1 sp, ch 1) around to last ch-1 sp, skip last ch-1 sp, work ending 2-dc Cluster.

Rnd 10: Ch 2, hdc in next ch-1 sp and in each Cluster and each ch-1 sp around; join with slip st to first hdc: 46 hdc.

Rnd 11: Repeat Rnd 2.

Rnd 12: Ch 1, sc in same st as joining and in next FPhdc, ch 3, (sc in next 2 sts, ch 3) around; join with slip st to first sc, finish off.

Ear Warmer

Ch 70; being careful **not** to twist ch, join with slip st to form a ring.

Rnd 1 (Right side)**:** Ch 2 **(counts as first hdc, now and throughout)**, hdc in next ch and in each ch around; join with slip st to first hdc: 70 hdc.

Note: Loop a short piece of yarn around any stitch to mark Rnd 1 as **right** side.

Rnd 2: Ch 2, work FPhdc around next hdc, ★ work BPhdc around next hdc, work FPhdc around next hdc; repeat from ★ around; join with slip st to first hdc.

Rnd 3: Ch 3 **(counts as first hdc plus ch 1, now and throughout)**, skip next FPhdc, ★ work 2-dc Cluster in next BPhdc, ch 1, skip next FPhdc; repeat from ★ around, work ending 2-dc Cluster: 35 Clusters and 35 ch-1 sps.

Rnds 4 and 5: Ch 3, (work 2-dc Cluster in next ch-1 sp, ch 1) around to last ch-1 sp, skip last ch-1 sp, work ending 2-dc Cluster.

Rnd 6: Ch 2, hdc in next ch-1 sp and in each Cluster and each ch-1 sp around; join with slip st to first hdc: 70 hdc.

Rnd 7: Repeat Rnd 2.

Rnd 8: Ch 1, sc in same st as joining and in next FPhdc, ch 3, (sc in next 2 sts, ch 3) around; join with slip st to first sc, finish off.

EDGING

With **right** side facing and working in free loops of beginning ch *(Fig. 1, page 44)*; join yarn with slip st in same ch as joining slip st; ch 1, sc in same st and in next ch, ch 3, (sc in next 2 chs, ch 3) around; join with slip st to first sc, finish off.

HINTS FOR WEARING
THE CUFF TURNED DOWN

Turn the cuff **wrong** side out.

Pull the cuff onto your leg with the top edge first.

Put on your boot, tucking the bottom edge of the cuff inside the boot.

Flip the top edge of the cuff over the top of the boot.

VERSATILITY SET

EASY

SHOPPING LIST

Yarn (Medium Weight)

[7 ounces, 364 yards
(198 grams, 333 meters) per skein]:

☐ Tan - 1 skein

☐ Black - 10 yards (9 meters)

Crochet Hooks

☐ Size L (8 mm) **or** size needed for gauge

☐ Size H (5 mm)

Additional Supplies

☐ Yarn needle

SIZE INFORMATION

Cuff - 5½" high x 12½" circumference (14 cm x 32 cm)

Ear Warmer - 4" wide x 18½" circumference (10 cm x 47 cm)

GAUGE INFORMATION

With larger size hook and holding two strands of yarn together,

   9 dc and 6 rows/rnds = 4" (10 cm)

Gauge Swatch: 4" (10 cm) square

With larger size hook and holding two strands of Tan together, ch 11.

Row 1: Dc in fourth ch from hook and in each ch across (**3 skipped chs count as first dc**): 9 dc.

Rows 2-6: Ch 3 (**counts as first dc**), turn; dc in next dc and in each dc across.

Finish off.

── STITCH GUIDE ──

TREBLE CROCHET

(abbreviated tr)

YO twice, insert hook in st indicated, YO and pull up a loop (4 loops on hook), (YO and draw through 2 loops on hook) 3 times.

INSTRUCTIONS
Cuff (Make 2)

Beginning at bottom edge, with larger size hook and holding two strands of Tan together, ch 28; being careful **not** to twist ch, join with slip st to form a ring.

Rnd 1 (Right side)**:** Ch 3 (**counts as first dc, now and throughout**), dc in next ch and in each ch around; join with slip st to first dc: 28 dc.

Note: Loop a short piece of yarn around any stitch to mark Rnd 1 as **right** side.

Rnds 2-7: Ch 3, dc in next dc and in each dc around; join with slip st to first dc.

Rnd 8: Ch 1; working from **left** to **right**, work reverse sc in each dc around (*Figs. 4a-d, page 46*); join with slip st to first st, finish off.

Bow (Make 2)

With smaller size hook, using one strand of Black, and leaving a long end, ch 3; join with slip st to form a ring.

Rnd 1 (Right side)**:** Ch 1, work (sc, hdc, dc, tr, dc, hdc, sc, ch 1) twice in ring; join with slip st to first sc, finish off leaving a 12" (30.5 cm) end.

Note: Mark Rnd 1 as **right** side.

Wrap the long end around the center of the Bow several times to form the knot; then tie the yarn ends in a knot on the **wrong** side of the Bow. Thread yarn needle with the ends and using photo as a guide for placement, sew Bow to **right** side of Cuff.

Ear Warmer

With larger size hook and holding two strands of Tan together, ch 42; being careful **not** to twist ch, join with slip st to form a ring.

Rnd 1 (Right side)**:** Ch 3 **(counts as first dc, now and throughout)**, dc in next ch and in each ch around; join with slip st to first dc: 42 dc.

Note: Mark Rnd 1 as **right** side.

Rnds 2-4: Ch 3, dc in next dc and in each dc around; join with slip st to first dc.

Rnd 5: Ch 1; working from **left** to **right**, work reverse sc in each dc around; join with slip st to first st, finish off.

Edging: With **right** side facing, holding two strands of Tan together, and working in free loops of beginning ch *(Fig. 1, page 44)*, join yarn with slip st in same ch as joining slip st, working from **left** to **right**, work reverse sc in each ch around; join with slip st to first st, finish off.

Bow

Work same as Cuff Bow, page 37; thread yarn needle with the ends and sew to **right** side of Ear Warmer.

Note: Each Option set uses an amount
of yarn that is slightly less than the Tan set.

Option #1:

Crochet the set using one strand **each** of Red and Black, working
through Rnd 7 on the Cuffs and Rnd 4 on the Ear Warmer.

Option #2:

Option #3:

Crochet the set using 2 strands of Green, working through Rnd 7 of the Cuff and through Rnd 4 of the Ear Warmer. Use buttons in place of the Bows.

Crochet the set using 2 strands of Maroon, working in Back Loops Only of each stitch through Rnd 7 on the Cuffs and through Rnd 4 of the Ear Warmer *(Fig. 2, page 45)*. Use buttons in place of the Bows.

GENERAL INSTRUCTIONS

ABBREVIATIONS

BPdc	Back Post double crochet(s)
BPhdc	Back Post half double crochet(s)
ch(s)	chain(s)
cm	centimeters
dc	double crochet(s)
FPhdc	Front Post half double crochet(s)
FPdc	Front Post double crochet(s)
hdc	half double crochet(s)
mm	millimeters
Rnd(s)	Round(s)
sc	single crochet(s)
sp(s)	space(s)
st(s)	stitch(es)
tr	treble crochet(s)
YO	yarn over

SYMBOLS & TERMS

★ — work instructions following ★ as many **more** times as indicated in addition to the first time.

( ) or **[ ]** — work enclosed instructions as many times as specified by the number immediately following **or** work all enclosed instructions in the stitch or space indicated **or** contains explanatory remarks.

colon (:) — the number(s) given after a colon at the end of a row or round denote(s) the number of stitches you should have on that row or round.

CROCHET TERMINOLOGY	
UNITED STATES	INTERNATIONAL
slip stitch (slip st) =	single crochet (sc)
single crochet (sc) =	double crochet (dc)
half double crochet (hdc) =	half treble crochet (htr)
double crochet (dc) =	treble crochet(tr)
treble crochet (tr) =	double treble crochet (dtr)
double treble crochet (dtr) =	triple treble crochet (ttr)
triple treble crochet (tr tr) =	quadruple treble crochet (qtr)
skip =	miss

CROCHET HOOKS

Metric mm	U.S.
2.25	B-1
2.75	C-2
3.25	D-3
3.5	E-4
3.75	F-5
4	G-6
5	H-8
5.5	I-9
6	J-10
6.5	K-10½
8	L-11
9	M/N-13
10	N/P-15
15	P/Q
16	Q
19	S

BEGINNER — Projects for first-time crocheters using basic stitches. Minimal shaping.

EASY — Projects using yarn with basic stitches, repetitive stitch patterns, simple color changes, and simple shaping and finishing.

INTERMEDIATE — Projects using a variety of techniques, such as basic lace patterns or color patterns, mid-level shaping and finishing.

EXPERIENCED — Projects with intricate stitch patterns, techniques and dimension, such as non-repeating patterns, multi-color techniques, fine threads, small hooks, detailed shaping and refined finishing.

Yarn Weight Symbol & Names	LACE 0	SUPER FINE 1	FINE 2	LIGHT 3	MEDIUM 4	BULKY 5	SUPER BULKY 6
Type of Yarns in Category	Fingering, 10-count crochet thread	Sock, Fingering Baby	Sport, Baby	DK, Light Worsted	Worsted, Afghan, Aran	Chunky, Craft, Rug	Bulky, Roving
Crochet Gauge* Ranges in Single Crochet to 4" (10 cm)	32-42 double crochets**	21-32 sts	16-20 sts	12-17 sts	11-14 sts	8-11 sts	5-9 sts
Advised Hook Size Range	Steel*** 6,7,8 Regular hook B-1	B-1 to E-4	E-4 to 7	7 to I-9	I-9 to K-10.5	K-10.5 to M-13	M-13 and larger

*GUIDELINES ONLY: The chart above reflects the most commonly used gauges and hook sizes for specific yarn categories.

** Lace weight yarns are usually crocheted on larger-size hooks to create lacy openwork patterns. Accordingly, a gauge range is difficult to determine. Always follow the gauge stated in your pattern.

*** Steel crochet hooks are sized differently from regular hooks–the higher the number the smaller the hook, which is the reverse of regular hook sizing.

GAUGE

Exact gauge is **essential** for proper size. Before beginning your project, make the sample swatch given in the individual instructions in the yarn and hook specified. After completing the swatch, measure it, counting your stitches and rows or rounds carefully. If your swatch is larger or smaller than specified, **make another, changing hook size to get the correct gauge**. Keep trying until you find the size hook that will give you the specified gauge.

FREE LOOPS OF A CHAIN

When instructed to work in free loops of a chain, work in loop indicated by arrow *(Fig. 1)*.

Fig. 1

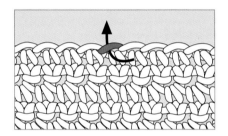

BACK LOOP ONLY

Work only in loop(s) indicated by arrow *(Fig. 2)*.

Fig. 2

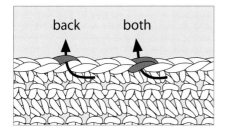

POST STITCH

Work around post of stitch indicated, inserting hook in direction of arrow *(Fig. 3)*.

Fig. 3

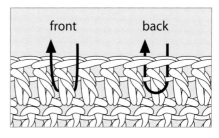

REVERSE SINGLE CROCHET

(abbreviated reverse sc)

Working from **left** to **right**, ★ insert hook in st to right of hook *(Fig. 4a)*, YO and draw through, under and to left of loop on hook (2 loops on hook) *(Fig. 4b)*, YO and draw through both loops on hook *(Fig. 4c)* (reverse sc made, *Fig. 4d)*; repeat from ★ around.

Fig. 4a

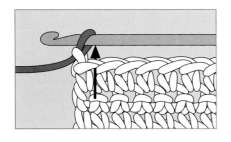

Fig. 4b

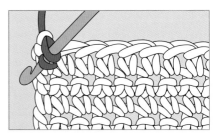

Fig. 4c

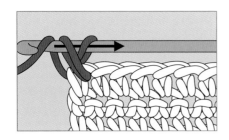

Fig. 4d

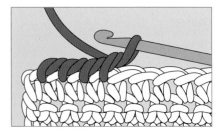

YARN INFORMATION

Each project in this leaflet was made using Medium Weight yarn. It is best to refer to the yardage/meters when determining how many balls or skeins to purchase. Remember, to achieve the finished size, it is the GAUGE/TENSION that is important, not the brand of yarn.

For your convenience, listed below are the specific yarns used to create our photography models.

CROSS STITCH SET
Caron® Simply Soft®
#9608 Blue Mint

IRISH SEA SET
Red Heart® Super Saver®
#0313 Aran

RIBBED SET
Red Heart® Super Saver®
#0336 Warm Brown

RUFFLED SET
Red Heart® With Love™
#1914 Berry Red

VERSATILITY SET
Red Heart® Super Saver®
Tan - #0360 Cafe Latte
Black - #0312 Black

OPTION #1
Red Heart® Super Saver®
Black - #0312 Black
Red - #0319 Cherry Red

OPTION #2
Red Heart® Super Saver®
#406 Med Thyme

OPTION #3
Red Heart® With Love™
#1914 Berry Red

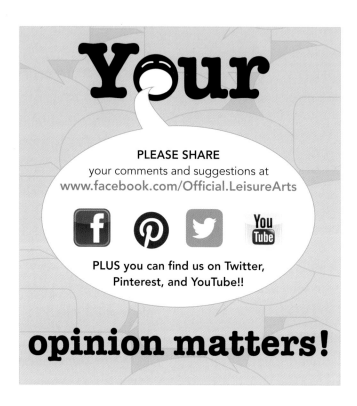

Your

PLEASE SHARE
your comments and suggestions at
www.facebook.com/Official.LeisureArts

PLUS you can find us on Twitter,
Pinterest, and YouTube!!

opinion matters!

We have made every effort to ensure that these instructions are accurate and complete. We cannot, however, be respnsible for human error, typographical mistakes, or variations in individual work.

Production Team: Writer/Instructional Editor - Sarah J. Green; Editorial Writer - Susan Frantz Wiles; Senior Graphic Artist - Lora Puls; Photo Stylist - Brooke Duszota; and Photographer - Jason Masters.